THE CHRIS...

Presented
to

_____

for

_____

THE CHRISTMAS GHOST

Robert Westall

Illustrated by
John Lawrence

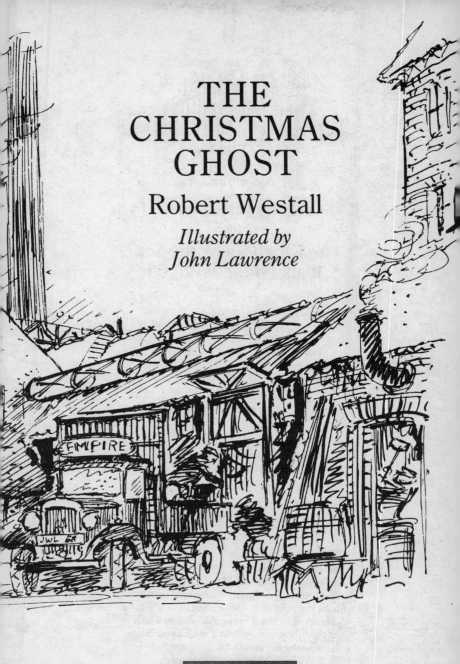

MAMMOTH

Also by Robert Westall

The Christmas Cat
If Cats Could Fly . . .
Size Twelve

for older readers

Falling into Glory
Gulf
The Kingdom by the Sea
A Walk on the Wild Side

First published in Great Britain 1992
by Methuen Children's Books Ltd
Published 1994 by Mammoth
an imprint of Reed Consumer Books Ltd
Michelin House, 81 Fulham Road, London SW3 6RB
and Auckland, Melbourne, Singapore and Toronto

ISBN 0 7497 1769 6

A CIP catalogue record for this title
is available from the British Library

Printed and bound in Great Britain
by Cox & Wyman Ltd, Reading, Berkshire

For my friend, Val Bierman
Thanks for all the haggis

Contents

CHAPTER ONE

Christmas Eve

My grownups were such marvellous *pretenders*.

The way my own grandmother would solemnly help me send messages to Santa, in the dark nights before Christmas. Sitting snug by her kitchen range, I would scrawl requests on strips she tore from the edges of our local newspaper. Then she would hold them over the glowing coals, let go, and they would fly up the sooty chimney like swift singed birds.

And then there was the way, last thing on Christmas Eve, that my mother would reverently set out a clean white cloth on the kitchen table, and put on it, for Santa, a brimming glass of port wine and a freshly baked mince pie. And in the morning, early, I would find the glass empty, with big thumbprints on it. Evidence, Sherlock Holmes, evidence! I would preserve the thumb-marked glass for days, like a holy relic.

And of course, as Christmas grew near, I would be seized with an expectation so great that I could hardly sit down long enough to eat my meals. It wasn't the presents themselves, though I liked them well enough. It was the fact that he was *coming*. That out there somewhere in the snowy dark was this utterly powerful being who knew all about me, and whether I'd been a good boy all year, and who meant to reward me with incredible gifts. I wonder I didn't get him mixed up with God. But Santa seemed more like God's kinder, merrier younger brother, who you might dare to speak to, if you were lucky enough to catch him on his rounds.

Of course, I had doubts. The size of box my clockwork train set had come in the previous Christmas made me wonder how Santa coped with just the lads in our street, let alone all the lads in the whole world. But I just thought that Santa was an expert, with hidden tricks of his own I couldn't begin to guess at. Just like my father, who was foreman-fitter at the chemical works, and who made me things at work, like a two-foot wooden model battle cruiser, or a full size machine gun on its own tripod. With a father like mine, I had no difficulty believing there were wizards in the world . . .

Anyway, by Christmas Eve, I would be prowling non-stop, like a tiger in its cage. My mother coped by sending me on errands. She seemed to have forgotten so many items, when normally she forgot nothing. A packet of icing sugar, half a pound of currants, tissue paper, string. Every one necessitating a journey. But I didn't mind. The dark green winter sky showed off our glowing snowbound town like black velvet showed off the diamond necklaces in the jeweller's. Barrows lined every pavement, their flaring acetylene lamps illuminating landscapes of things never seen at other times. The banked sleekness of chestnuts, the silver globes of wrapped tangerines, pink exotic pomegranates and coconuts with faces like shrivelled monkeys.

And the butchers, with their rows of birds hanging like dead, plump, naked chorus girls,

with just a frill of feathers at their neck, and
their last agony only showing in the clenching
of their feet.

And the shoppers, pirouetting like living
Christmas trees, so laden with parcels as
they turned and turned, calling their
greetings as they passed each other.

'Aall–the–best–hinny–how's–your–Ernie –
good–can't–stop–now–Aah've–still–got–so–
much–to–do–and–he's–on–the–six–till–two–
shift–so–Aaah'm–doing–it–all–myself–this–

year.' Such glad exhaustion, jubilant
desperation . . .

Only in the dark background, unflustered,
unhurried, without hope, the unemployed
men, squatting silent on their haunches, spat
into the gutter with the accurate hate of a
German sniper on the Somme. I turned my
eyes away from them, as I always ran past
the gate of the fever hospital with my mouth

shut, holding my breath. Bad luck was infectious too.

Such was my morning. After a gobbled lunch, there were the rituals to witness. The icing of the cake and the sticking upon it of the little robin redbreast with tiny springs in place of legs, so that if you flicked him in passing, he rocked for ages. (I flicked him too hard one year, and he flew across the room and I got a clout, though not a hard one.)

Then the lettering on the mirror over the fireplace, in whitewash:

MERRY CHRISTMAS TO ALL

My mother, once a fruiterer's assistant, paints with the same elegant script in which she once announced on the fruiterer's window:

BEST COXES 6D A POUND

I am allowed to add the snowflakes; I always put on too many and my mother wipes half of them off with the hem of her apron.

Then the hanging of the decorations, my mother whimpering instructions with her mouth full of drawing pins. Then the blowing up of balloons; my lungs are very small, but my father has shown me how to

do it, rubbing the balloon between my palms, and warming it at the fire. But still it usually gets away by blowing my own air back into my own lungs, or making delicious farting noises, or escaping altogether to whizz round the room like a miniature rocket, and end up sadly on the fire, and we only have six of them. And lastly the Chinese lanterns, with their real candles, which are always hung too close to the door-lintels, so that the smell of singeing varnish is as much a Christmas smell as the aroma of my uncle's cigars.

None of these rituals will I let my mother omit, down to the tiniest detail. It is all part of the Coming of Santa . . .

And suddenly it is time for the family to be calling. And, of course, it is essential that I greet them a good two hundred yards from home, and skip wildly around them all the way, like a destroyer escorting a convoy. In fact, if they are very late, I have been known to greet them as they left their own front doors . . .

First my God-hating Aunt Rosie, basket full of newbaked mince pies, under a white cloth. I walk alongside her and

reach slyly under the cloth and nick a
mince pie. Still so hot it burns my mouth,
while she walks along, with a tolerant
smile on her face, noticing and not
noticing. Tolerant of everyone, my Aunt
Rose. Of everybody except God.

'Prince of Peace?' she snorts, settling
herself on our couch. 'What peace? That
Mussolini bombing little bairns to bits in
Abyssinia? Why doesn't God strike him
dead? And that poor young lass three
doors down from me, four little mouths to
feed an' her husband dying of TB in

Preston Infirmary. What kind of Christmas is it going to be for *her*?'

For half an hour, the desolations of the world, carefully saved up for Christmas Eve, would flood our kitchen. Then she, too, suddenly brightening, would say, 'Merry Christmas, all the best, hinny!' and depart.

And then out into the dusk again, my eyes searching for the distant beloved dumpy figure of Nana, with the Christmas bird under her arm, its white unplucked feathers glinting as she passes under the street-lamp. Those feathers will soon fill the air of our kitchen, like upward-drifting snow; still cling in soft tufts to her bare brawny arms, as she reaches deep inside the bird and produces the glistening coils of pink and brown that are the mystery of the bird's inner life. And I look at the bird's face and wonder how it feels to have your insides dragged out, even if you are dead. The bird's eyes are tight shut; it looks patient and bored stiff and trying not to notice.

Nana likes to make a drama of it. 'That's the gall bladder,' she points out with gusto. 'If that bursts afore you get it out, the whole bird's ruined.' And she gives the greeny oval object an extra-dangerous squeeze for good measure, poised over the gaping belly, before dropping it safely in the bin.

Once she tried holding a white feather to my nose, as if threatening me. I must have simply looked puzzled.

'You're not like your dad then?' she said at last, very disappointed. 'Your dad was terrified of feathers when he was a bairn. He was so scared of a feather he used to wet himself.'

I couldn't believe that my dad, who was afraid of nothing, could ever be scared of a little white feather. I didn't believe her, and said so. When my father got home, she held a feather under his nose, and he stirred backwards uneasily, saying, 'Give over, Mother!'

Today, though, she is again disappointed.

'Isn't he in?'

'He's on the two till ten shift.'

'That's what Aah thowt. Only I Aah saw his bait there, with his tea-makings . . .'

'Oh, dear, he's forgotten them . . .'

They both look at me. I am delighted.
Another errand. The best errand in the
world. My father is an oily wizard, and I
am going to see him in his enchanted
kingdom.

'Run along, chick,' says my grandmother. 'He'll be gasping for his brew o'
tea.'

CHAPTER TWO

Otto's Kingdom

Off I run. In one hand his sandwiches, knotted in their huge red spotted handkerchief. In the other, his blue enamel tea can, with its curious hedgehog-ball of condensed milk, sugar and dry black tea leaves, to which he will add a scalding jet of water, from one of his great glowing hissing boilers.

In the dusk, the shopping crowds are thinning, but still exultant.

'Give Tommy me best!'

'See you Boxing Day!'

In a side street, church carol singers are singing "It came upon a midnight clear". One year, when I was little, they came and sang at our house, after I'd fallen asleep. I wakened, thinking they were the angels; full of joy to know the Christmas angels really existed.

But my mind was elsewhere now; on the great works of the Empire Chemical Company that filled the western horizon of the town, decorating the last of the red sunset with a hundred long plumes of smoke and steam, black, grey, blue, even red where the upward glow from an open furnace suddenly lit them.

Of course, nobody ever called it the Empire Chemical Company. Everybody called it Otto's. Otto had started it, sixty years ago. In our lads' minds, he still stalked the town. Great huge dark Otto, with his broadbrimmed hat and his beard dangling halfway down his chest. It was a good joke to borrow your dad's trilby hat, and grab your mam's smallest doormat and hold it under your chin, and run at your mates booming, 'Otto, Otto!' Otto Liebner, Otto the Jew, fabulous monster. People hated him when he first came, to make soda lime and soda ash. They thought he would use the Leblanc Process, which filled the air with green acid fumes and killed the grass and trees for miles around. People thought they were going to be choked to death in their own beds. They gave him a rough time. The kids threw dog turds at him. The men at the railway station made sure that the spare parts he ordered got lost. Then a boiler blew up and boiled three men alive. They said after that that Otto was unable to sleep; he walked the works night and day, a demon in a nightmare. To get the men to stay at their work, after their mates died, he dozed in the very place of disaster, nodding off in his huge caped greatcoat.

And then it all came right. His process, the Solvay Process, was clean and killed nothing. No more boilers blew up. After three years, Otto pronounced, 'We are not making soda ash, we are making gold!'

After that, he couldn't do enough for the town. He was the first to give the workers a fortnight's paid holiday. Public library, public baths, mechanics' institute, co-op store, new buildings for the grammar school I hoped to go to soon, all were Otto's.

A man of the people, my father said. Walked round the works all day, didn't lurk in any old office. Any worker could say anything he liked to him. But he'd felled three at once, when they got too stroppy . . .

And then he got old, so that in his great house, he had to have a lift built to take him upstairs . . . and now he was a dead hero, buried in London. But Otto's town still prospered, even in the Great Depression. Some might be out of work, but not so many as in Sunderland, or Jarrow.

The works were still deadly, mind. Men still got killed, if they were careless. Boiled or roasted or fried. My dad had once to dismantle a coke crusher, to get a body out. He said the man's shoulders had jammed the machine, but his head was gone. That was all he ever said, except the man had been a heavy drinker, even at work . . .

So now I was heading for Otto's kingdom, which was also my father's. Past the twelve-foot wall, with glass set in the top to keep the fools out. Up to the gate, and the timekeeper's office.

I hated the timekeeper. He was not a proper man; he never got his hands dirty, my father said. What was more, he was bossy. If he saw me coming, he would grab me into his office and summon my father by phone, turning a little handle with petty vigour. He would drag my father from his work; which my father hated. And he would keep me out of the works, which *I* hated.

I peeped round the corner at him. He sat lounging at his long counter in waistcoat and

shirtsleeves, with his flashy brass armbands to keep his cuffs high on his wrists and clean. Dark curly hair, and a little dark moustache on his pudgy face. Reading the evening paper. Call that a job, reading the paper, when my father was risking his neck, high on the gantries, like a proper man?

I bent double, and tiptoed across the cast-iron weighbridge that lay in front of his office. I was nearly there when my tea can clanked on the iron. He jumped out of his doze, and shouted, 'Hey.'

But I was flying off into the works, where he daren't follow me. He dared not leave his little office.

Through the dusk I ran. Up the cobbled streets on which lay great lakes of water, swirling with the slick exciting patterns of oil and petrol. I skipped between them, running up thin isthmuses of cobbles, leaping from island to island to keep my best Christmas Eve shoes clean. Breathing in great lungfuls of benzol, and the lovely choky gas from the coke, that made your lungs fizz and your head spin. Rats ran from me, squeaking into corners. Pipes stuck out of walls all over the place, puffing out little clouds of green gas with a chuffing noise, or dribbling strange thick fluids like a kid with a snotty nose. In places, the very brickwork was rotting, as patches of white or blue or green climbed up into it from out of the ground.

There was hidden life everywhere. The ground vibrated under my leather soles, to the thump of the crushers. High up among the girders, a little siren wailed, and someone clanged a huge steel door in reply,

and there was the terrifying avalanche rumble of falling stone, banging into metal.

Every open door showed me a scene. A blacksmith with the clenched face of a fiend in the glow of his furnace, beating fat pink sparks from a lump of white glowing metal. The stables where the carthorses lived; huge movement in the dark; a slow chomping; the clink of a horseshoe, as a horse changed its weight from one leg to another; the sweet smell of hay and oats, and the lovely sweaty smell of dusty horse and rancid horse pee.

I put down my things for a moment on the

windowsill, and nipped inside to have a word with old Maisie, old Ruby. Oh, the pebbly cold sweetness of a horse's nose, the huge mystery, in the gloom, of a dark shining horse's eye!

Then up with my things again and on, into the wondrous depths of Otto's kingdom, my father's kingdom, *my* kingdom . . .

'Yes, son? What you want?'

A man in overalls, blackened face, shining teeth and eyes. A proper man, one of my father's mates, a friend.

'Oh,' he said, 'it's Jack's lad, isn't it?' And my heart swelled with pride, at being Jack's lad.

'Let's find him then!'

And we went from man to man. 'Jack's lad's here. With his bait. Know where Jack is?'

Shouts echoing through the din.

'Think he's up number two crusher!'

'He was here, but he's gone down the bagging plant!'

'Try the limestone tower. Number three!'

My father is everywhere and nowhere, like God. Keeping the whole world running, as he would say, smooth as a Swiss watch.

We reached the base of the incredible soaring limestone tower. The figure with the black face turned to me.

'Have to leave you here. Know your way?'

CHAPTER THREE

The Lift

Oh, what it is to be trusted! Up all those endless iron stairs, which had holes in their treads so that you saw the ground below, moving beneath your feet in the most lovely and terrifying way . . .

'You'd better use the lift . . . it's down . . . look, there, with the little light inside it.'

I gasped; the ultimate privilege. For this was Otto's lift.

Waste not, want not was the motto in those days. As soon as he was dead and didn't need it any more, it was ripped out of his great house and installed in the limestone tower to save the workers' legs.

All the kids round the town said it was

haunted. My father said that was rubbish. It was just that it was a funny place to put it, 'cos it was all grand and rich and fancy, in that gaunt and rusty place.

Anyway, there was no arguing. The man pushed me in and closed the doors behind me and I pushed the button, polished bright by so many thumbs, and the lift started to grind slowly and uncertainly upwards, like it was ill and dying itself.

I stood and stared around me. It was certainly the most odd thing to find in such a place. It was of the most beautiful red mahogany, still polished up near the ceiling (though *very* dusty) but scarred and worn by men's boots and bodies further down. The plaster ceiling was all encrusted with leaves and flowers, but cracked and brown with fumes and fag smoke. And there were mirrors set all around, in the top half of the walls. But not ordinary mirrors; they had bevelled edges, and were cut, again, with the most intricate whirling patterns of flowers and leaves, so you could hardly see your face in them at all. I tried pulling faces at myself, moving my head around so the patterns in the glass cut my head into funny shapes. Then I got tired of that, and wrote my name in the dust on the mahogany. Then rubbed it out quickly again, in case my father saw it.

The floor had been pretty floral tiles, but they were half worn away as well, and covered with footprints in dried grey mud. And a seat ran all round the lift, of dark red plush but threadbare and oilstained now, except in the corners. I thought it was a shame, that such a spoilt rich pretty thing should have to end its life in such a place. Like some lovely racehorse pulling a coal cart.

The lift seemed to be taking forever. It would have been quicker to climb the stairs. I just hoped it wouldn't break down and leave me stuck . . .

Then I went back to pulling faces again . . .

It was then I saw the other face, in the mirror. Behind me. It made me jump, I can tell you. All alone in that little confined space, where I thought I'd been by myself.

Then I laughed out loud. Because it was the face of Santa Claus; the fat face with the bright red cheeks, the white hair, the long, curly, snowy beard, the tiny dark eyes, half-buried in fat. Somebody must have

pinned up a Christmas card, for the festive season!

I spun round to look at the card.

It wasn't there. I couldn't see anything but the dusty mahogany walls, the patterned ceiling, the scarred floor and the worn seats of red plush.

Nothing.

Oh, c'mon I thought. There has to be a sensible explanation. It must be all these patterns cut in the mirrors that's doing it. And my imagination. I had a terrible imagination. Once I came running home crying, saying that I'd seen a poor dead cat in the street, that had been run over, and all its guts were hanging out. I mean, I hadn't dared go nearer to it than ten yards, but I'd seen its eyes and ears, and the blood. My father went out with me, for he was fond of cats. Then he began laughing and dragged me up to it, and it was nothing but a crumpled wet old jacket, that somebody had tossed down as rubbish.

So I turned back to the mirror, angling my head this way and that, trying to make it do again what it had done before. And then I found a clear two inches of mirror and . . .

Got the face again. I just thought it funny that Santa wasn't wearing his red cap. Just his snowy hair . . .

And then the face moved; changed its expression. It didn't turn all evil or anything. Just desperate and terrified.

Again I spun round. And there was nothing there.

Then the lift arrived at the top with a bump and a bang, and a little bell rang, and I was struggling to get that lift door open like a mad thing, with the tea tin still clutched in one hand, and the red bait-hanky in the other.

'All right, all right, hold your horses,' said a cross voice. 'What's the hurry? Where's the bloody fire?'

It was my father's voice, and that calmed

me. Then he got the lift doors open from the other side, and I more or less fell into his arms.

He held me away at arm's length, and surveyed me coolly.

'Oh, you've brought me bait,' he said. 'What's the rush? Think I might starve to death?'

The men behind him laughed, but not cruelly. Just the way men will laugh at a young lad, when they're in a good humour.

Then he said (for he was no fool where I was concerned): 'What's upset ye?'

And I was so beggared to know what I should say, how I should explain, that I made a shruggy joke of it.

'Thought I saw Santa Claus in the lift.'

If I thought I would get a laugh, I was very wrong. There was a sudden awful silence.

'What d'you mean?' asked my father sharply. 'Santa Claus in the lift?'

'Just an old bloke with white hair and a beard an' rosy cheeks. He looked a bit like Santa.'

'You mean, he came up wi' you an' got off halfway?'

'That'll only be old Sammy Dawes,' said one of the men behind him, as if anxious to close the subject. 'Only he's got a white moustache not a beard. He is a bit like Father Christmas, is old Sammy.'

'Nobody got on with me,' I said. 'And nobody got off the lift halfway. This was just a face I saw in the mirror. An old guy with rosy cheeks and white hair and beard.'

'Strewth,' said one of the men behind my father.

And another muttered a word that sounded like 'Otto'.

'Only,' I said, 'I thought he was a Christmas card somebody had pinned up on the wall. Then I saw his face move. But when I turned round, there was nobody there . . .'

The silence, on top of that high tower, deepened, so that I heard the soft sighing of the breeze through the girders, and somewhere a loose piece of corrugated iron flapped and banged, making me jump.

'A white beard an' rosy cheeks,' muttered one man.

'It's him,' muttered another. 'How did he look, son?'

'Terrified,' I said. 'Desperate.'

I could tell from the look on my father's

face that he was suddenly terribly angry with me. He could've hit me, though he was never the hitting sort.

'It's him,' said the first man again. 'It's old Otto.'

'Come to warn us. There's goin' to be a death in the plant tonight.'

'Don't talk so bloody wet,' snapped my father. 'That's nothing but old wives' tales.' He turned on the man who had spoken. 'Have you got nothing better to do? D'you think this plant runs itself?'

'Bloody wet, nowt!' said the man defiantly. 'Davy Nessworthy saw old Otto that night afore Billy Stansfield fell into the crusher. In the lift. In the mirror. Didn't you, Nesser?'

'Aye, Aah did.' Davy Nessworthy was small but determined, not to be put down. He glared at my father harder than my father glared at him.

'You're worse than a pack of old women,' shouted my father. 'Get back to work, afore I sack the lot of you. And think on what you're doing, or somebody *will* get killed by carelessness. Keep your minds on your work.'

'You'll check up on things, Jack?' Little

Nesser asked my father. 'Keep your eyes open? We don't want some woman widowed on Christmas Eve . . .'

My father looked at them. Even I could see they had the wind up, and my father knew them better than I did. He said, his voice going a bit gentler, 'I'll keep my eyes open. I'll check up on things, like I always do. Have I let you down yet? And don't go phoning every part of the works, the moment me back's turned, making them nervous. I want everybody to have a merry Christmas . . .'

They murmured again, a little placated. Then he turned to me.

'I'll see you out of the gate. You've caused me enough worry for one night.'

'Don't be hard on the lad, Jack,' said Little Nesser. 'He only said what he saw. How could he know what old Otto looked like?'

My father made a sound of exasperation deep in his throat; half a grunt and half a snarl, almost the noise men make before they spit. Then he shoved me into the lift in front of him.

I didn't see anything in the mirrors on the way down. I didn't even dare look into them, with his eye on me. I kept my own eyes on the worn, ornate footprinted tiles on the floor.

He marched me to the gate, his hand on my elbow, almost like I was under arrest. Then gave me a shove out into the night; and nodded to the dozy timekeeper.

'That your lad?' said the timekeeper, nervously. 'I thought it was him sneaking in. But he was too quick for me.'

'You're too slow to catch cold,' said my father, his anger still hovering. Then he called after me, 'Straight home, mind! Tell your mam I won't be late.'

CHAPTER FOUR

Black Widows

I ran off in relief that it hadn't been worse. As I said, my father wasn't a hitter; but he was a brooder. If I incurred his disgust, he sometimes wouldn't speak to me for days. A thunderstorm hung over the house. Sometimes I wished he'd hit me and get it over with.

But as I slowed to a walk, before I got a stitch in my side, I started to worry. All the things the men had said kept going round in my mind. Little Nesser was right. I hadn't known what old Otto had looked like, in the last years of his life. To me, as to all the lads, he was a huge striding figure with a big black beard. So how could I have invented the pathetic little Santa of the mirror?

43

And Little Nesser had seen him, the night Billy Stansfield fell into the crusher . . .

And . . . the word 'widow' kept going round and round in my mind. I knew the widows from the works. They walked round our town, always in black, never smiling, carrying some terrible burden so I sometimes crossed the road to avoid them. Their faces were so still, as if nothing was ever going to happen again in their lives except the bearing of the burden. And their kids had the same still expression; they were not *normal*. They were no good at school work or games. They didn't even *try*. And they might suddenly burst out crying without warning, horrible crying that went on and on. They were like bombs waiting to explode. You never played with them; never went calling for them at their houses. When you had to go to their back doors, on an errand for your mam, you noticed their houses smelt funny. We all thought it was the smell of death . . .

Somewhere in the town there was some ordinary woman, busy getting ready for Christmas, humming carols, tying up presents, getting the bird stuffed, all happy . . .

Who would be a widow by morning.

For the rest of her life.

I thought about God, waiting and watching and letting it happen. Sitting up there above the clouds, listening to all the carols being sung in his praise, sending out the angels to Bethlehem to proclaim tidings of great joy to men of goodwill, and letting some poor beggar at Otto's get himself fried to death by molten soda ash, or boiled alive in a vat of caustic till the flesh came off his bones like the Christmas turkey's.

I knew there was no point to praying about it, like I used to pray about passing my exams, or being bullied by David Black. God did do small favours. But my aunt was right. He wouldn't do anything about this. It was his business, not my business.

And it was no good asking Santa. All that poor silly sod could do was go on giving out presents; so some kid would get presents and a boiled-alive dad. And my father would do his best, would check everything like he always did. But he hadn't been able to stop Gordon Stansfield's dad falling into the crusher . . .

And then the terrible thought struck me that it might be my dad who copped it. He might be foreman, but that wouldn't save him if some pipe burst and the steam shot out. In fact he'd be in more danger than all the rest, because he would prowl around till the end of his shift looking for the cause of trouble, walking into danger. Like a man stalking a tiger.

And then my mam would be a widow and wear black and walk round with a still, frozen face for the rest of her life. And I would turn rotten at school work and sport, and nobody would want to play with me any more . . .

I turned a corner, and walked into the middle of the Sally Army. They had given up promising Hell to drunkards for one night in the year, and were playing "Once in Royal David's city . . ."

I nearly threw up in the gutter there and then. The thought of the comfort of home, the curtains drawn and the coal fire blazing up the chimney and the dog snoozing in front of it, and me mam happily frying sausage and chips for tea, our usual Christmas Eve treat . . . and my Nana getting the bird into the oven to roast until it was brown and crisp . . .

I couldn't go home. Home was a warm and cosy trap, with nothing to think about but

worry about me dad.

I hovered on the kerb, listening to the
Sally Army and staring down at a broken
beer bottle in the gutter.

And then it came to me.

There was one thing that could help; there was one thing that knew what was going to happen.

The face in the mirror.

I knew now it had been trying to tell me something. Warn me in time.

I had to go back. I had to go back and face it, and work out what it was trying to say.

God, if I got caught this time, my father would kill me. He'd skin me alive. He wouldn't speak to me for a month, and he'd think I'd done it to make a fool of him in front of the men. He might never speak to me for the rest of my life.

But I'd rather have him not speaking to me than have him in a black coffin, roasted like a Christmas turkey. At least he'd still be alive . . .

I started to run back towards the works. Then I slowed to a walk. It wouldn't do to arrive panting and shaking. The timekeeper would hear me coming a mile off.

CHAPTER FIVE

The Return

Everything seemed to go wrong. I decided, when I got near the gate, to take my shoes off so my steel heel and toe caps wouldn't click on the iron weighbridge. I took them off, and tied them together and hung them round my neck. Then, bent double, I started to cross and discovered too late what I should have remembered, that the weighbridge itself was studded with squares of iron an inch across, that pressed into my bare feet like torture implements. By the time I got to the far side, my feet were agony. Then I discovered that the bows I'd tied in my shoelaces had turned into knots, tight knots. I had to cower in a dark tunnel that led off to the right, trying to untie the knots in the dark. And the knots were tight, and my mam had just cut my fingernails after my Christmas bath . . .

It seemed to take me half an hour, and all the time the rats were squeaking about and running across my feet and I was scared they'd bite me with their poisonous fangs and I was expecting a crash or a bang, or a flash or a scream, and to hear the work's siren hoot out its terrible emergency hoot that told the whole town that some poor devil had copped it.

I got my shoes on again at last, and headed for the limestone tower, which seemed to fill the sky, the light of the works' street lamps staining it upwards with a dim glow.

And there seemed to be men everywhere now. They were no longer my allies. They mustn't see me, or they'd send for Dad. I seemed to have to cower in every doorway. And the men didn't just walk past now whistling, like they usually did; they gathered in groups near me, and muttered in frightened voices, and I knew what they were talking about. In spite of my father's orders, the word about Otto had got around. And I grew afraid that by spreading that word, by spreading panic, I was going to

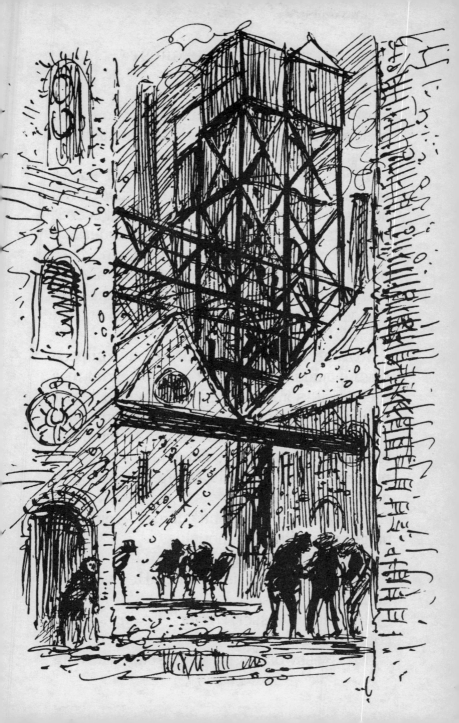

make the accident happen. When one of the men got into a tizz and made a fatal mistake. And it would be all my fault . . .

I died a thousand deaths, before I got to the foot of that tower. And then saw to my horror that the lift wasn't there. I could see it motionless, high up among the girders. I would have to wait for it to come down.

It was five minutes before I remembered you could summon lifts by pressing the button; so you can see what kind of state I was in.

It came at last. The door began to open, when I suddenly realised to my horror that there was somebody inside. And no ghost either. Two big black-faced men with jangling tea cans. It was too late to hide. If I ran, they'd chase me. So I just stood and nodded to them, as I had often seen them nod to each other.

'Thought you'd gone home,' said the bigger man, friendly enough.

'I forgot something,' I said.

'Your dad's not up there. He went to number four crusher.'

'It's Little Nesser I want,' I said, staying cool somehow.

'Mr Nessworthy to you, son,' said the

bigger man severely. Then they nodded and went away. And holding my breath, I got inside the lift, closed the doors and pressed the big brass button, still kept shiny by the constant pressure of men's thumbs.

The lift began to slowly jerk upwards. And my eyes flicked from mirror to mirror, in a mixture of desperate hope and total disbelief. I mean, it was such an odd place. I saw mirror within mirror within mirror. And all dim and entangled in the mass of cut glass, overlapping foliage of flowers and stems and leaves. I could see the front of my face and the back of my head in the same mirror. And if I looked sideways, I could see myself, a whole row of me standing like a row of soldiers standing to attention, curving away into forever . . . how could I find what I wanted to know in that endless maze?

'C'mon,' I said desperately. 'C'mon. There's not much time.' As I would to another kid.

And then suddenly, I knew he was in the lift with me.

Not in the mirrors. In the lift itself, sitting behind me. And as I turned, I shut my eyes, afraid that I would see him. And when I did see him, through near-shut eyes, a wave of

shock hit me, as if I'd been standing in the shallows on a beach, and it had been an icy wave of the sea.

He sat, in the far corner. I still have the crazy impression that the seat sagged a little under his heavy bulging thighs. He looked so solid and real, you see. The slightly greasy folds of his waistcoat, with its heavy gold watch and chain. His boots, highly polished but old and cracked, as if they were a favourite pair of boots he could not bear to part with. The carnation in his buttonhole, that showed up so frighteningly fresh and young, against the dying sagging yellow of his face. The length of his white beard, stained brown with tobacco at each side of his mouth. The white hair that made him look like Santa Claus in the mirror; the rosy cheeks that I could now see were an unhealthy network of broken veins.

The lift was full of the smell of old man, like the smell of my grandfather's house. The lift was full of the sound of his breathing, as he pressed his heavy-fingered pudgy hand against his side, as if to stem some tide of pain. His mouth was open, and black inside.

But he didn't frighten me. His face was agonised; but kind. I was only scared he would die again at any moment, before my very eyes, before he could tell me what I had to know.

'Where?' I managed to gasp out. 'Where's the . . .'

He understood. His eyes looked right, towards one corner of the lift, one corner of the whole limestone tower. Then, unable to speak for his gasping, he raised both pudgy hands in the air and brought them down with a scissors movement, making a diagonal cross in the air. And then he really did begin to die, and I couldn't bear to look.

But when I heard the lift clang home at the top I looked again. And he was gone. And the smell.

★   ★   ★   ★

Somebody opened the lift doors, and I practically fell out, breathing in the coke-tainted air as if it was the freshest I had ever breathed.

'Where's Mr Nessworthy?' I said.

'Here, son, here.' Little Nesser came forward and grabbed me before I fell, as the high gantries rocked around me against the dark sky.

'You've seen him again?' asked Little Nesser, his sooty greasy face very close to mine.

'Aye,' I gasped. 'He showed me where the danger was. I think. He nodded *that* way.' I nodded my head in the direction of one corner. 'And he made a sign like *this*.' I feebly sketched the sign in the air, wondering if anyone would understand.

Nesser frowned. Then he said, 'The cross-stanchion! By God, the cross-stanchion. If that's going, we're all dead men.'

CHAPTER SIX

Five Minutes to Midnight

It was too much for me. I must have fainted, and I was glad to faint. Except that they told me afterwards that I nearly fell through the safety-railing, and if Little Nesser hadn't grabbed me, I'd have fallen two hundred feet. But I didn't know anything of that. Only my ears were still working, as I heard someone whirling the handle on the telephone, and Little Nesser's voice yelling for my father to come. And, a bit later, I came round and saw my father being lowered over the railing on a thick rope, with a big torch in his hand. His last act was to take off his greasy old cap and hand it to one of his mates, as if it was something precious. And I watched through the holes in the metal

58

walkway and saw his tiny lamplit figure
dwindle and dwindle, until he landed with his
feet on a great X of concrete that made him
look no bigger than an ant. I saw him kick at
the concrete with his steel-tipped boot. And
the concrete exploded and fell away in
fragments out of the lamplight. And I heard

Nesser say, 'He's signalling. Close the tower down. *Close her down.*'

And a bell rang, and the biggest, nearest rumbling ceased, and it almost seemed like a total silence.

Then I heard Nesser say, 'Bring him up, lads. Very slow and easy.'

Then my father climbing back over the rail, saying, savagely, 'The concrete's rotten. Rotten as dry shit. The reinforcing rods are rusted through. Get everybody out of here.'

They sent me down with the first liftful.

★　　★　　★　　★

They sent me home in the shift-manager's car, a little Austin Seven. Everybody seemed to want to help me into it; hands kept touching me and patting me on the back or the shoulder. I hardly noticed the journey home; the houses and street lamps were just a whirl in the dark.

The driver kept on telling my mother that I'd saved lives. My mother kept on saying that she hoped I'd behaved myself and not done any harm. Then she put me to bed and brought an enamel bowl of warm water and

bathed my face and hands very gently, and I complained about being put to bed early on Christmas Eve.

I must have fallen asleep by the time my father got home. What woke me was the way the bed sagged, when he sat down on it; and his comforting smell of coke fumes and fag smoke, that never really left him, however often he had a bath.

'You awake?'

'Aye.'

'They've closed the whole works down. Frightened the vibration'll finish off the limestone tower. It's hanging by a bloody thread o' metal. I'd never have guessed that cross-stanchion would go. The fumes must a' rotted the concrete; it's only thirty years old . . .'

'Wasn't your fault,' I said stoutly.

'No. Aah've only got charge o' the moving parts. Civil engineer's fault, who built it. He's probably dead years ago. Feller called Chapman.'

There was a long silence then.

Then, he said, 'Lucky Little Nesser spotted it. I'll not ask what you thought you were doin' there . . .' More silence, and sounds of my father struggling with his beliefs. Finally he said, 'Otto died in that lift, you know. His heart gave out, poor old beggar.'

'I thought he died in London.'

'No, he was buried in London. But he died in that lift.'

I remembered the dying agonised face.

My father sighed, as if it was all too much.

'He never got over those first three men getting scalded. It preyed on his conscience, they say. He was never happy after,

however much money he made. He was a good feller in his own way. True to his lights.' Then he added savagely, 'It's coming to something when little bits o' bairns have got to be used to put the world to rights.'

Then he got off the bed. He would say no more. Ever.

'Merry Christmas, Dad!'

He pulled out his watch, from the pocket of his coat, and squinted at it, in the dim light from the hall.

'Hold your horses. It still wants five minutes to midnight. Save it for the morning.'

And then he was gone.